Land of
Ice and Snow

Contents

From Pole to Pole
   The Arctic 4
   Antarctica 6
Animals of the Ice and Snow 8
   Polar Bears 10
   Emperor Penguins 12
Exploring the Arctic 14
Racing on Ice 16
Living in the Ice and Snow 18
The Coldest Town on Earth 20
Exploring Antarctica 22
Against the Odds 24
World Park Antarctica 26
Really Cool Art 28
Glossary 30
Index 31
Discussion Starters 32

Features

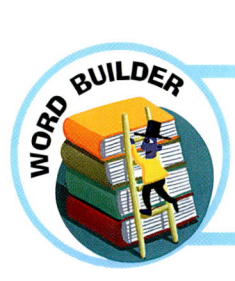

WORD BUILDER

Do you know what to put in front of some words to make an opposite? Turn to page 7 to learn the opposite of the word *arctic*.

IN FOCUS

What in the world do giant bears of the north and giant birds of the south have in common? Find out on pages 10–13.

PROFILE

This man led his crew to safety in one of the greatest polar adventure stories of all time. Discover more in **Against the Odds** on page 24.

EARTH WATCH

What do you think happens to rubbish in the freezing temperatures of Antarctica? Read how scientists learn more about Earth on page 27.

SITESEEING · PEOPLE & PLACES

What was in the diary of Robert Falcon Scott?

Visit **www.infosteps.co.uk**
for more about **EXPLORERS OF THE ICE AND SNOW**.

From Pole to Pole

The two polar regions of the world are unusual and beautiful places, frozen with ice and snow.

The Arctic

The North Pole lies at the far-northern tip of our planet. An ice-covered ocean is surrounded by frozen land called **tundra** that lies beneath a blanket of snow for most of the year. This part of the world is called the Arctic.

When temperatures fall as low as -53°C, as they can do in the polar regions, boiling water freezes as soon as it hits the air. It explodes into ice shards.

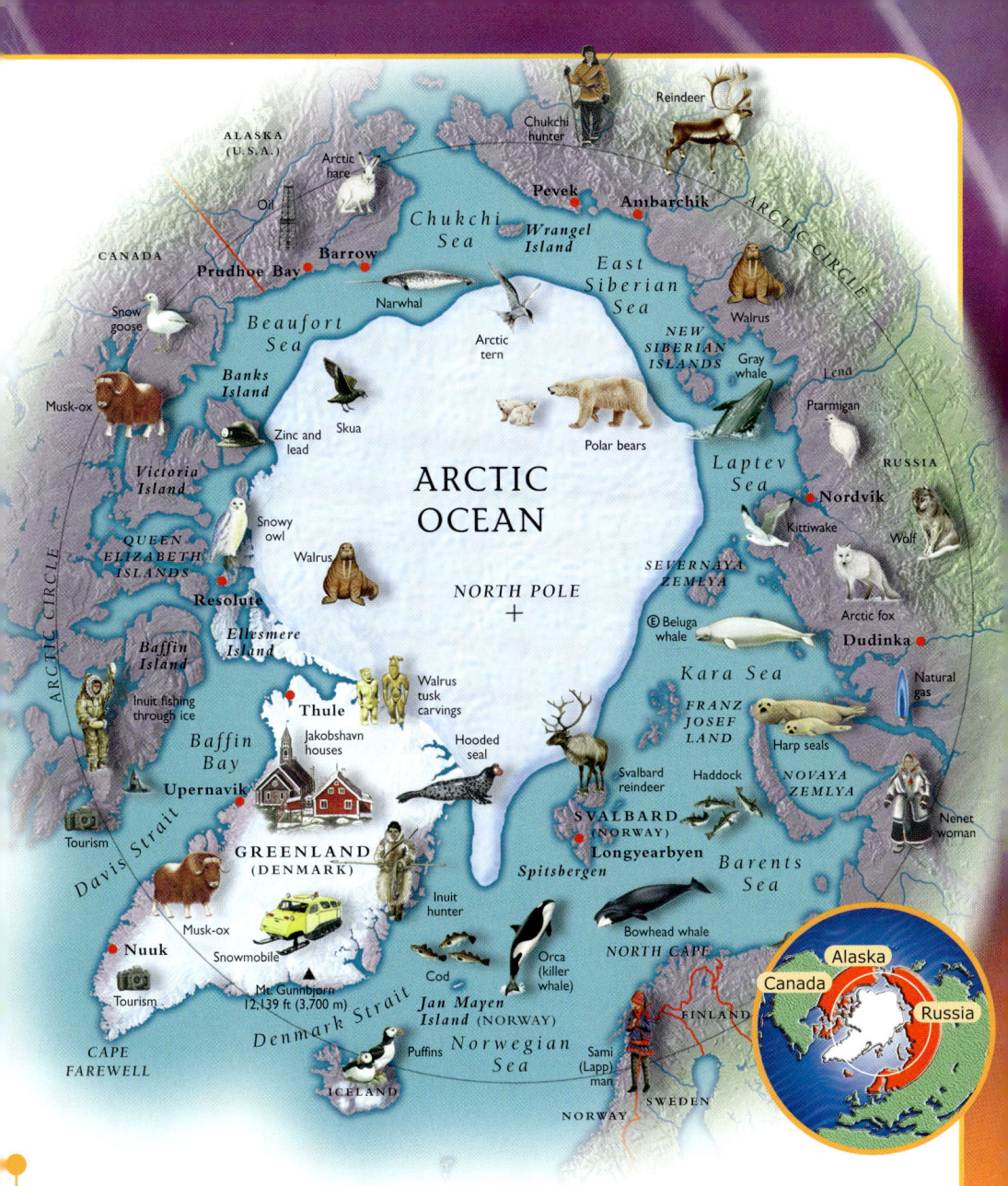

The Arctic is bordered by an imaginary line called the Arctic Circle. Countries of the Arctic Circle are sometimes called "lands of the midnight sun". In midsummer it is light almost 24 hours of the day. The sun shines even at midnight. In midwinter it is dark for this amount of time.

5

Antarctica

At the opposite end of Earth lies the continent of Antarctica. This includes the South Pole. Antarctica is the coldest and iciest place on our planet. Ice, several kilometres deep in parts, covers all but a few rocky windswept valleys and the tops of the highest mountains.

Huge **glaciers** spill down the mountains and flow into the oceans surrounding Antarctica. These are frozen solid for much of the year. Sometimes enormous chunks of ice split off and become floating icebergs.

From Pole to Pole continued

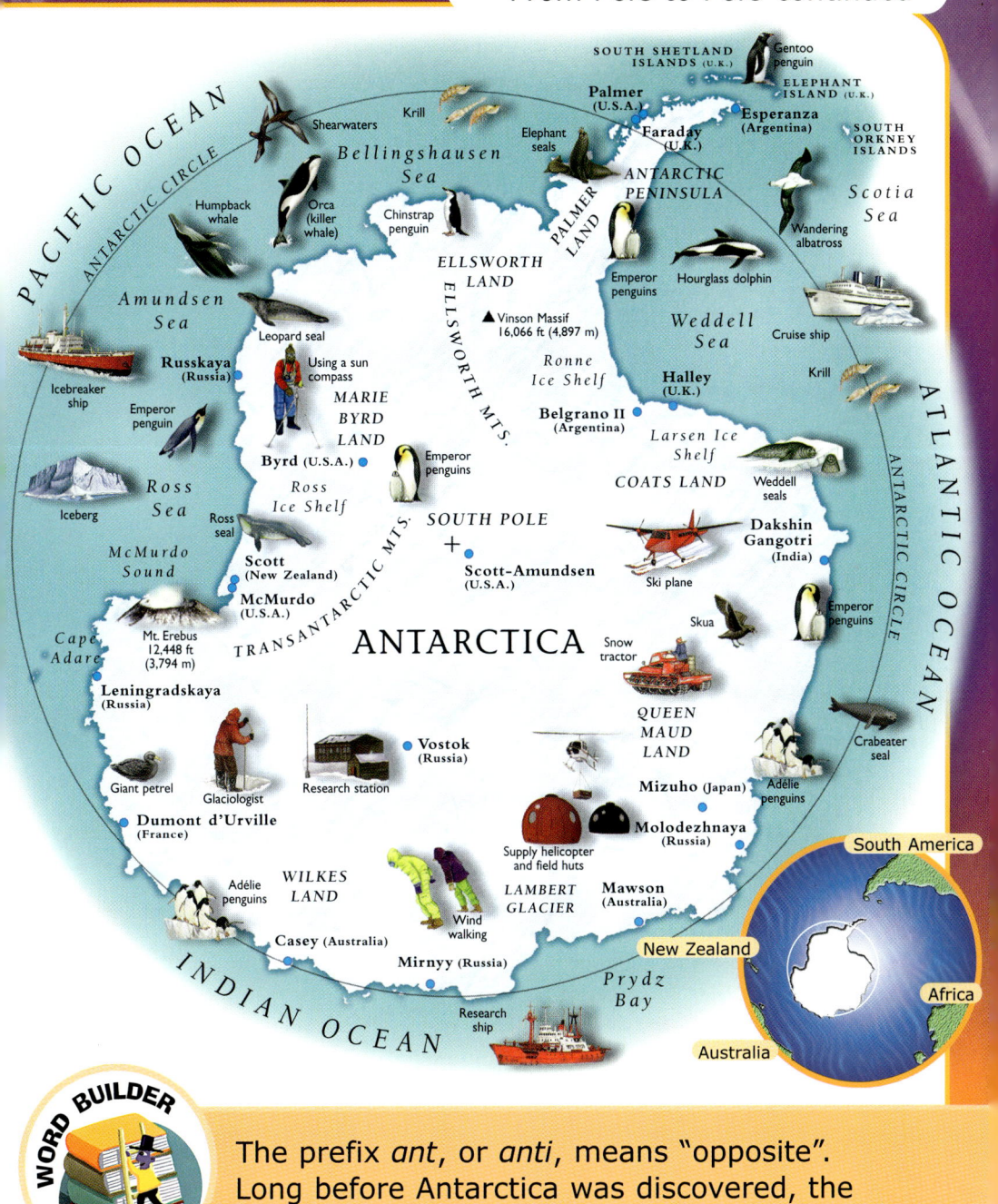

ANTARCTICA

WORD BUILDER

The prefix *ant*, or *anti*, means "opposite". Long before Antarctica was discovered, the ancient Greeks predicted that there must be a great southern land to balance the land in the north. They were right. *Antarctica*, or the *Antarctic*, is at the opposite end of Earth as the *Arctic*.

7

Animals of the Ice and Snow

Many animals are able to live in very cold climates. Some animals spend all year in the ice and snow. Many Arctic animals change colour as winter approaches. They grow thick white coats that blend well with the snow, making them difficult to see. Others huddle together or curl up into small tight balls against the bitter cold.

Some animals hibernate through the winter, living off their stored fat and saving energy by staying still. Others, like the caribou, **migrate** to warmer places as winter sets in.

Musk oxen have the longest hair of any mammal. Their thick shaggy coats keep them warm in the icy Arctic weather.

Red fox

Humpback whale

Polar bear

Snowshoe hare

Key 🔵 Arctic animals
🔵 Antarctic animals

Snowy owl

Emperor penguins

Leopard seal

Lynx

Caribou

9

IN FOCUS

Polar Bears

Polar bears are the giants of the bear family and the largest predators on land. They are well suited to life in the freezing Arctic. A layer of fat keeps them warm in the icy water where they hunt seals. Polar bears are excellent swimmers.

A Year of a Polar Bear

1
2
3
4

Animals of the Ice and Snow continued

● Where polar bears live

① For most of the year polar bears live out on the ice that covers much of the Arctic. Their white fur and skin absorbs sunlight for warmth.

② In late autumn a female polar bear builds a snow den where she sleeps away the winter months. In midwinter she gives birth to cubs.

③ In spring the mother bear brings her cubs out into the open. The cubs stay with their mother for two years.

④ The mother bear protects her cubs and teaches them how to hunt seals.

IN FOCUS

Emperor Penguins

Emperor penguins live in Antarctica. They are expert swimmers. On land they stay warm in the icy **polar desert** by huddling together in colonies.

Emperor penguin chicks hatch during the cold bleak Antarctic winter. The mother penguin lays an egg, which the father penguin looks after. He holds the egg on his feet and keeps it warm under folds of fat. The mother penguin then begins a long march to the ocean to feed. She returns two months later when the chick hatches. The father penguin eats nothing this whole time.

metres
1.2
0.9
0.6
0.3
0

| Emperor | Chinstrap | Yellow-eyed | Magellanic |

Animals of the Ice and Snow continued

The mother and father penguin both look after the chick and bring it food. Groups of chicks huddle together while their parents are at sea hunting for fish.

There are 17 kinds of penguins. Emperor penguins are the largest of all and can grow as tall as a seven-year-old child.

Fjordland   Little (Fairy)

Exploring the Arctic

Inuit people have made the Arctic areas of Alaska, Canada and Greenland their home for thousands of years. They are experts at living in the freezing conditions. Long ago Inuit people lived by hunting fish, seals, whales and deer. They trained teams of dogs called huskies to pull sleds as they moved from place to place.

It wasn't until the 1900s that the first European explorers reached the Arctic and discovered the North Pole. They learned how to stay alive in the ice and snow from the Inuit people.

In the early 1900s explorers from many countries were racing to be the first to reach the North Pole. An American named Robert E. Peary was the first to get there in 1909.

For Peary it was a case of third time lucky! His first two attempts failed. Success cost him seven years of hard work and eight of his toes which he lost to **frostbite**!

15

Racing on Ice

People are racing for first place in the Arctic ice and snow to this day. Each year in the wilderness of Alaska, the most popular winter race of all time takes place. It is the Iditasport. Athletes choose their own human-powered transportation—skis, bikes or feet. They trek 210 kilometres through Alaska in the dead of winter following tracks more suited to moose than people. They must complete the course in less than 72 hours.

The Rules

1. The Iditasport is a dangerous race. Every racer must sign a special form.
2. The same method of transport must be used for the whole distance.
3. No motorized vehicles are allowed.
4. Racers must sign in at each checkpoint.
5. Every racer must carry camping equipment the whole distance. (This includes a sleeping bag, a lighting system, and a water-making system.)
6. No littering is allowed.
7. Racers can file a protest against anyone seen breaking the rules.
8. The race director can disqualify a racer at any time.
9. There are NO TIES!

Living in the Ice and Snow

Many people live in the far-northern lands of ice and snow. In Arctic areas such as Lapland there are many modern cities and towns. People combine old and new ways of life. In some places the Saami people of Lapland still farm herds of reindeer. The deer are very important for their milk, meat, hides and bone.

In Lapland, green, red and gold lights blaze across the sky during winter. These northern lights are called the Aurora Borealis and they are one of nature's most beautiful light shows!

The Aurora Borealis can be seen in many Arctic Circle countries, but some people say the show is best in Lapland!

The colourful national costume that the Saami often wear honours their family and ancestors.

The Coldest Town on Earth

The coldest town on Earth lies within the Arctic Circle in Siberia, Russia. Here human breath freezes into ice crystals in an instant and the frozen ground cracks and bangs like thunder.

Life goes on for the people of the town of Verkhoyansk, even though winter temperatures can drop to -51°C. The children simply dress in warm coats, scarves, fur hats, mittens and reindeer boots to do their chores and go to school!

Lena Potapova thinks Verkhoyansk is the coolest town! She doesn't mind having to break up blocks of ice for her family's water supply.

Lena walks five minutes to school and bundles up to fetch blocks of frozen milk from the local store.

Verkhoyansk

● Russia

Exploring Antarctica

There are no native people of Antarctica. Because this great southern land of ice and snow is so far from any other land mass, it was not discovered until the 1800s. It wasn't until later that the first explorers set foot on the continent. When they did the race for the South Pole was on!

Many great explorers from many different nations set off on long dangerous **expeditions** to the South Pole. On December 14, 1911 the Norwegian explorer Roald Amundsen and his team became the first people to reach the South Pole.

James Cook    Robert Scott    Ernest Shackleton    Roald Amundsen

Time Line of Early Antarctic Explorers

1772–1775	Captain James Cook **circumnavigates** Antarctica.
Early 1800s	Seal hunters from many different countries explore the oceans and islands around Antarctica.
1901–1904	The first British National Antarctic Expedition is led by explorer Captain Robert Falcon Scott. The men set up a base.
1907–1909	A British expedition led by Ernest Shackleton travels to within 156 kilometres of the South Pole, but is forced to turn back because of bad weather.
1910–1911	Norwegian explorer Roald Amundsen and his team become the first to reach the South Pole on December 14, 1911.
1910–1912	Scott's party reaches the South Pole on January 17, 1912 to find the Norwegian flag flying. Scott and his companions die on the return trek.
1914–1916	Sir Ernest Shackleton returns with his team in the *Endurance* on a quest to cross Antarctica from coast to coast. They are caught in **pack ice**.

SITESEEING · PEOPLE & PLACES ·

What was in the diary of Robert Falcon Scott?

Visit www.infosteps.co.uk
for more about EXPLORERS OF THE ICE AND SNOW.

Against the Odds

"MEN WANTED:
for hazardous journey. Small wages, bitter cold, long months of complete darkness, constant danger, safe return doubtful. Honour and recognition in case of success. Sir Ernest Shackleton"

Sir Ernest Shackleton

Would you want a job like this? When the great explorer Sir Ernest Shackleton (shown centre) placed the ad above in a London newspaper in 1914, twenty-seven men signed up for the job. They were officers, sailors, surgeons, biologists, geologists, cooks, photographers and more.

Ernest Henry Shackleton was born in Ireland in 1874. He died in 1922.

With his team Shackleton set off on an expedition to cross the unmapped continent of Antarctica. The plan went wrong when his ship, the *Endurance*, became stuck on thick pack ice and sank. This left the men stranded in the freezing conditions. Against all odds Shackleton led his crew to safety in an astonishing story. He is remembered as one of the world's greatest leaders.

World Park Antarctica

The journeys of early explorers helped people learn about Antarctica. Today scientists from all over the world have research stations in Antarctica. They go there to explore and study. Their work can affect the fragile environment, however, so people are thinking of ways to keep Antarctica safe.

In 1959 twelve countries signed a special agreement called the **Antarctic Treaty**. They agreed to protect Antarctica and decided to use it only for peaceful projects. Today many more countries have signed the treaty and Antarctica is a park for the world to share.

EARTH WATCH

In Antarctica temperatures can drop to as low as -89°C. Visitors to Antarctica must be careful to leave no waste behind because nothing decomposes in the icy conditions.

27

Really Cool Art

Nature carves beautiful sculptures in the ice and snow of Antarctica. Wind and water are always at work making new shapes each day.

A world away in the cold lands of the north, people work hard to make sculptures of their own. During winter carnivals great blocks of ice are cut and shaped into grand palaces and artists carve chunks of ice into life-sized figures and scenes.

This ice palace in northern China glows from the inside out! It is lit by neon tubes of purple, pink, blue and green.

29

Glossary

Antarctic Treaty – an agreement that allows people to use Antarctica for peaceful projects only. Members of the Antarctic Treaty protect the plants, animals and resources of Antarctica. Scientists agree to share research.

circumnavigate – to go all the way around

expedition – a long journey with a special purpose. During the early 1900s many brave explorers crossed Antarctica on great expeditions.

frostbite – when parts of the body freeze. Explorers of the ice and snow must protect themselves from frostbite because it can badly damage body parts such as fingers and toes.

glacier – a huge slab of slow-moving ice. Glaciers are found in polar regions and in high mountains where they carve out *U*-shaped valleys.

migrate – to move from one place to another

pack ice – huge chunks of frozen sea water that have been crushed together to form a floating mass of ice

polar desert – an area of dry frozen land where hardly any snow falls

tundra – flat treeless land where the ground is frozen almost all year long

Index

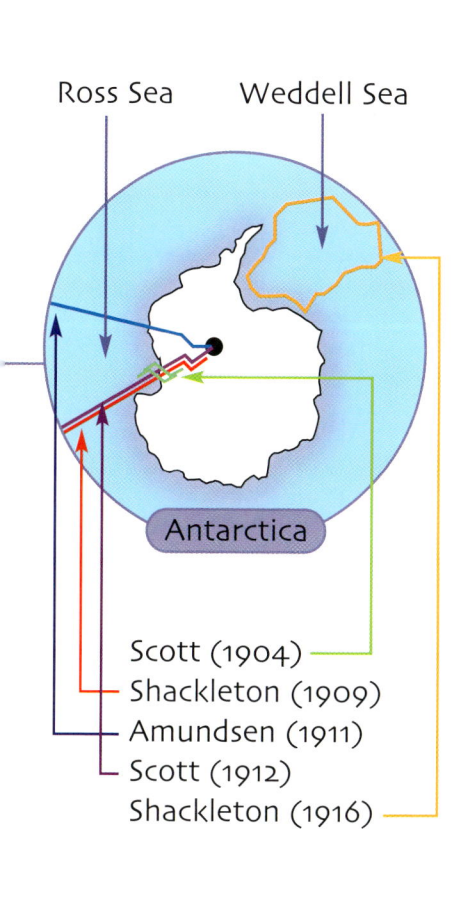

Amundsen, Roald	22–23
Antarctica	6–7, 9, 12, 22–28
Antarctic Treaty	26
Arctic	4–5, 8–11, 14–16, 18, 20–21
Aurora Borealis	18
Cook, Captain James	23
huskies	14
Iditasport	16–17
Inuit	14
Lapland	18–19
North Pole	4–5
Peary, Robert E.	15
penguins	9, 12–13
polar bears	9–11
reindeer	18–19
Saami	18–19
Scott, Captain Robert Falcon	23
Shackleton, Sir Ernest	23–25
South Pole	6–7, 22–23

Discussion Starters

1 Take a look at the whooper swans on the cover of this book. They have stopped to rest during their long journey south and are snuggled up in a blanket of snow. How could you find out more about these amazing high-fliers?

2 If you were going on a long journey over dangerous land and in freezing conditions, how would you plan your trip? What sort of person would you need to be?

3 The Antarctic Treaty is one example of how people from many countries work together for the good of all. Can you think of other groups that work in this way?